Tracking Jack

Following Kerouac to Desolation Peak

MICHAEL MCCARTHY

RED APPLE
PUBLISHING

Copyright © 2015 Michael McCarthy
First printing May 2015
Cover design and text layout: Jim Henry
Cover photo: Michael McCarthy
Inside photos Michael McCarthy
ISBN: 0994753241
ISBN-13: 978-0994753243

DEDICATION

This book is dedicated to all those fans of the writing of Jack Kerouac who have somehow managed to keep his name, spirit and books alive after all these years. Whatever chord Jack struck within our hearts, that feeling still remains almost half a century after his passing.

.

CONTENTS

ACKNOWLEDGMENTS

Thanks to the *North Cascades Institute* for keeping the spirit of the northwest wilderness alive with their creative and inspiring programs that teach people of all ages about this magnificent region, and for hosting me on my explorations of the Cascades. Thanks to NCI for originating the idea for the *Poets on the Peaks* program in the first place. The spirit of poet Gary Snyder, the original "back to the land" prophet, still permeates the air in these mountains. My thanks to the *Environmental Learning Centre* for the fine accommodation, well designed and maintained buildings, dining and service.

The *Poets on the Peaks* program was led by (retired) Park Service ranger and natural storyteller Gerry Cook, who has a wealth of tall tales about the mountains, the fire lookout where he himself served for a summer season, Jack Kerouac and Kerouac's fans, the Cascades wilderness, Ross Lake, and for his piloting of the remarkable landing craft the Ross Lake Mule. Those who make the steep 6,000-foot ascent of Desolation Peak with Gerry are lucky people indeed.

The National Park Service does a remarkable job of maintaining the facilities at the wilderness campgrounds and on the trails. Seattle City and Light are to be thanked for allowing the public to access their properties and for offering boat tours of Diablo Lake. I'm appreciative of Tom Barnett at Ross Lake Resort taking the time to speak with me about his knowledge of the lake, mountains, weather and trails. Congrats to John Suiter for writing and publishing the definitive guide to the Beat poets and their legacy in this region in his excellent book *Poets on the Peaks*.

A mention goes to Lawrence Ferlinghetti and City Lights bookstore for keeping the Kerouac and Beat Generation legacy alive by stocking and selling their books, and for providing another pilgrimage site for Kerouac fans at his store in North Beach, San Francisco. The book was laid out by Jim Henry of Red Apple Publishing, who deserves a word for his ghostly book cover design. Finally, a big hello and shout out to all those Kerouac fans who have kept Mad Jack's spirit alive for all these years. I'll see you on the way to the trail up Desolation Peak.

.

THE RUCKSACK REVOLUTION

"I see a vision of a great rucksack revolution, thousands or even millions of young Americans wandering around with rucksacks, going up to mountains to pray..."

So how does a writer described as "mediocre at best" by many literary critics and whose name has been virtually forgotten somehow manage to still influence more young people than any other writer before or after his time? One of the most enduring American novels of all time, On the Road appears on virtually every list of the 100 greatest American novels ever written. Jack Kerouac may have more fans today than at any time during his short and spectacular career. How does this compute? What gives?

Let me confess. I am still one of those dedicated fans. I first read Jack Kerouac at the impressionable age of 14. I had always wanted to be a writer and had just finished with the explorations of Jack London and was working my way through the bluff machismo of Ernest Hemingway when I stumbled across On the Road. I was dumbfounded. I immediately went on to read most of Kerouac's books while in high school and college. At the same time Bob Dylan released his masterpiece Like a Rolling Stone, directly influenced – as Dylan has said – by his own discovery of On the Road.

The song's most famous lines can actually be seen as a summation of On the Road, espousing the sense of Kerouac's personal isolation from mainstream America. "How does it feel to be on your own, with no direction home, like a complete unknown, like a rolling stone?" To many of us who heard those lines at the time, well, the feeling wasn't all that great. Many young people rejected mainstream American culture and values, or at least they played at rejection, for a while. Others truly felt and lived that sense of isolation. Personally, I took Dylan's question to heart and went out on the road myself to look for answers.

While some kids my age were marching in the streets and protesting (before graduating and getting a nice job with a fat pay cheque and eventually a wife and kids, that is) others hit the road with a vengeance, looking for something more meaningful than three square meals a day and a comfy couch. On the Road became a bible for we restless wanderers. I was living in Montreal at the time. I stuck out my thumb and somehow ended up in Vancouver. I hitched around North America for several years, hopping freights and sleeping in Sally Ann's and hippie communes and farmer's fields and telephone booths.

What the hell was I looking for? Maybe I was searching for the ghost of Jack Kerouac and his sidekick, the eternal speed freak whackball Neil Cassidy. Put together the two were every good mother's worst nightmare, wild hipsters looking for kicks and getting high and running away from responsibility and searching for the eternal fountain of youth and salvation that didn't exist for hipsters any more than it did for the savage Spanish conquistadors. I was on it myself.

I've seen Kerouac on YouTube on old TV shows from the early sixties and to tell the truth he didn't look very charming or compelling on some, like the William Buckley Show. Being shitfaced drunk on TV isn't cool, and TV is a cool medium. You don't want to look angry or crazy either. There is even no single book, sentence, poem or paragraph that Kerouac ever wrote that made me want to become a fan, but I was hooked on his incredible vision of a better tomorrow. Maybe it was this one line from the Dharma Bums that caught my attention: "I see a vision of a great rucksack revolution, thousands or even millions of young Americans wandering around with rucksacks going up to mountains to pray…"

To my mind, this quote presages the hippie generation that came directly after the Beats. Kerouac's time on Desolation Peak was directly due to Gary Snyder, an outdoorsman and poet and student of Zen who had become involved with the Beats literary scene in San Francisco. Drugs and drunkenness and revolution were not part of Snyder's lifestyle. Snyder had little in common with Neil Cassidy and William Burroughs and Gregory Corso and other wild men who were part of the Beat scene.

Snyder went to Sourdough Mountain fire lookout in the North Cascades Wilderness, as far from civilization as you can get, to chop wood and meditate and write poetry. It was really Snyder who launched the ensuing hippie "back to the land" movement that came after the Beats, with its emphasis on escaping big city craziness and finding nirvana in nature. For one brief summer, Snyder took Kerouac

2

away from the urban madness to an isolated existence that allowed Kerouac a brief time of reflection and clarity. When Jack came down the mountain, On the Road was published and the rest is history.

These days it's Kerouac who still sells hundreds of thousands of books, not the soft spoken and philosophical Zen poet Snyder. It is Kerouac, with his railway brakeman outfit of white undershirt, khaki pants and boots who shaped the original cool hipster image, an image that over time sold hundreds of millions of blue jeans. Kerouac died in 1969, a lost and broken soul, yet blue jeans still fly off the retail shelves today in his forgotten memory. Movie stars Marlon Brando and James Dean copied that look and it shaped their own rebel images and made them famous. For them it was a fashion statement or marketing strategy. For Kerouac, it was just his work gear.

Why does Kerouac still maintain so many fans and a reputation that approaches idolization, and so much abiding respect among so many readers, if not literary critics who brush him off as a one-note wonder? The simple answer is: I don't know. This book is not going to provide you with any mystical answers in that regard. It is simply a guide to a path to a destination that few Kerouac fans even know exists, a place of pilgrimage where you can pay your respects to the madman, a living shrine to which you can travel – albeit in armchair comfort without having to climb that goddam steep mountain yourself. Hey, that's 12,000 feet of vertical gain and descent in one day we are talking about, and very hard just to access the starting point. I have the blisters to prove it.

As the hippies that followed in Jack's eternal footsteps used to say: Life? Hey, it's all a trip, man! This Desolation Peak cabin can be argued to be the location where all that other stuff started. Mad Jack, crazy Jack, we all love you and miss you. See you in heaven.

HISTORY OF THE BEATS

The Beat Generation was a group of American post-World War II writers who came to prominence in the 1950s, as well as the cultural phenomena that they both documented and inspired. Central elements of "Beat" culture: rejection of received standards, innovations in style, use of illegal drugs, alternative sexualities, an interest in examining religion, a rejection of materialism, and explicit portrayals of the human condition.

*This definition of the Beat Generation (above) is excerpted from Wikipedia.

Allen Ginsberg's *Howl* (1956), William S. Burroughs's *Naked Lunch* (1959) and Jack Kerouac's *On the Road* (1957) are among the best known examples of Beat literature. Both *Howl* and *Naked Lunch* were the focus of obscenity trials that ultimately helped to liberalize publishing in the United States. The members of the Beat Generation developed a reputation as new bohemian hedonists, who celebrated non-conformity and spontaneous creativity.

The original "Beat Generation" writers met in New York. Later, in the mid-1950s, the central figures (with the exception of Burroughs) ended up together in San Francisco where they met and became friends of figures associated with the San Francisco Renaissance. In the 1960s, elements of the expanding Beat movement were incorporated into the hippie and larger counterculture movements.

It is reported that Kerouac introduced the phrase "Beat Generation" in 1948 to characterize a perceived underground, anti-conformist youth movement in New York. The name arose in a conversation with writer John Clellon Holmes. Kerouac allows that it was street hustler Herbert Huncke who originally used the phrase "beat in an earlier discussion with him. The adjective "beat" could colloquially mean "tired" or "beaten down" within the African-American community of the period and had developed out of the image "beat to his socks" but Kerouac appropriated the image and altered the meaning to include the connotations "upbeat", "beatific", and the musical association of being "on the beat."

Burroughs had an interest in criminal behavior and got involved in dealing stolen goods and narcotics. He was soon addicted to opiates. Burroughs' guide to the criminal underworld (centered in particular around New York's Times Square) was small-time criminal and drug-addict Herbert Huncke.

Ginsberg was arrested in 1949. The police attempted to pull Ginsberg over while he was driving with Huncke, his car filled with stolen items Huncke planned to fence. Ginsberg crashed the car while trying to flee and escaped on foot, but left incriminating notebooks behind. He was given the option to plead insanity to avoid a jail term, and was committed for 90 days to Bellevue Hospital.

Beat writers and artists flocked to Greenwich Village in New York City in the late 1950s because of low rent and the 'small town' element of the scene. Folksongs, readings and discussions often took place in Washington Square Park. Allen Ginsberg was a big part of the scene in the Village, as was Burroughs. Burroughs, Ginsberg, Kerouac, and other poets frequented many bars in the area.

Allen Ginsberg moved on to San Francisco and began writing *Howl*. Lawrence Ferlinghetti of the City Lights Bookstore started to publish poetry in 1955. At a public reading Ginsberg performed the first part of *Howl*. It was a success and the evening led to many more readings by the now locally famous Six Gallery poets. It was also a marker of the beginning of the Beat movement, since the obscenity trial for Howl in 1957 brought it to nationwide attention.

The Beats also spent time in the Northern Pacific Northwest including Washington and Oregon. Kerouac wrote about sojourns to Washington's North Cascades in *The Dharma Bums* and *On the Road*. Portland, Oregon was also a locale for some of the Beat poets. Gary Snyder studied anthropology there, Philip Whalen attended Reed College, and Ginsberg held multiple readings on the campus around 1955 and 1956.

Kerouac's 1958 novel *The Dharma Bums* names its chief protagonist as "Japhy Ryder." a character who is actually based on Gary Snyder. Kerouac was impressed with Snyder and they were close for a number of years. In the spring of 1955 they lived together in Snyder's Mill Valley cabin. Most Beats were urbanites and they found Snyder almost exotic, with his rural background and wilderness experience, as well as his education and Oriental languages.

Snyder moved to Japan in 1955, in large measure in order to intensively practice and study Zen Buddhism, one of the primary subjects of *The Dharma Bums*, the book that undoubtedly helped to popularize Buddhism in the West and remains one of Kerouac's most widely read books.

The Beats had a pervasive influence on rock and roll, including the Beatles, Bob Dylan and The Doors. In fact, the Beatles spelled their name with an "a" partly as a Beat Generation reference, and John Lennon was a fan of Jack Kerouac.

Bob Donlon, Neal Cassady, Allen Ginsberg, Robert La Vigne and Lawrence Ferlinghetti

Ginsberg later met and became friends of members of the Beatles. Ginsberg was a close friend of Bob Dylan and toured with him in 1975. Dylan cites Ginsberg and Kerouac as major influences. Jim Morrison cited Kerouac as one of his biggest influences, and fellow Doors member Ray Manzarek has said: "I suppose if Jack Kerouac had never written *On the Road*, The Doors would never have existed."

Jack Kerouac; A Life in Letters

Born on March 12, 1922, in Lowell, Massachusetts, Jack Kerouac's writing career began in the 1940s, but didn't meet with commercial success until 1957, when *On the Road* was published. The book became an American classic that defined the Beat Generation. Kerouac died on October 21, 1969, from an abdominal hemorrhage, at age 47.

Jack's Early Life

Famed writer Jack Kerouac was born Jean-Louis Lebris de Kerouac on March 12, 1922, in Lowell, Massachusetts. A thriving mill town in the mid-19th century, Lowell had become, by the time of Jack Kerouac's birth, a down-and-out burg where unemployment and heavy drinking prevailed. Kerouac's parents, Leo and Gabrielle, were immigrants from Quebec, Canada; Kerouac learned to speak French at home before he learned English at school. Leo Kerouac owned his own print shop, Spotlight Print, in downtown Lowell, and Gabrielle Kerouac, known to her children as Me mere, was a homemaker.

Kerouac later described the family's home life: "My father comes home from his printing shop and undoes his tie and removes [his] 1920s vest, and sits himself down at hamburger and boiled potatoes and bread and butter, and with the kiddies and the good wife."

Jack Kerouac endured a childhood tragedy in the summer of 1926, when his beloved older brother Gerard died of rheumatic fever at the age of 9. Drowning in grief, the Kerouac family embraced their Catholic faith more deeply. Kerouac's writing is full of vivid memories of attending church as a child: "From the open door of the church warm and golden light swarmed out on the snow. The sound of the organ and singing could be heard."

Kerouac's two favorite childhood pastimes were reading and sports. He devoured all the 10-cent fiction magazines available at the local stores, and he also excelled at football, basketball and track. Although Kerouac dreamed of becoming a novelist and writing the "great American novel," it was sports, not writing, that Kerouac viewed as his ticket to a secure future. With the onset of the Great Depression, the Kerouac family suffered from financial difficulties, and Kerouac's father turned to alcohol and gambling to cope. His mother took a job at a local shoe factory to boost the family income, but, in 1936, the Merrimack River flooded its banks and destroyed Leo Kerouac's print shop, sending him into a spiral of worsening alcoholism and condemning the family to poverty. Kerouac, who was, by that time, a star running back on the Lowell High School football team, saw football as his ticket to a college scholarship, which in turn might allow him to secure a good job and save his family's finances.

"Some people are so poor, all they have is money"

Literary Beginnings

Upon graduating from high school in 1939, Kerouac received a football scholarship to Columbia University, but first he had to attend a year of preparatory school at the Horace Mann School for Boys in Brooklyn. So, at the age of 17, Kerouac packed his bags and moved to New York City, where he was immediately awed by the limitless new experiences of big city life. Of the many wonderful new things Kerouac discovered in New York, and perhaps the most influential on his life, was jazz. He described the feeling of walking past a jazz club in Harlem: "Outside, in the street, the sudden music which comes from the nightspot fills you with yearning for some intangible joy—and you feel that it can only be found within the smoky confines of the place." It

was also during his year at Horace Mann that Kerouac first began writing seriously. He worked as a reporter for the Horace Mann Record, and published short stories in the school's literary magazine, the Horace Mann Quarterly.

The following year, in 1940, Kerouac began his freshman year as a football player and aspiring writer at Columbia University. However, he broke his leg in one of his first games and was relegated to the sidelines for the rest of the season. Although his leg had healed, Kerouac's coach refused to let him play the next year, and Kerouac impulsively quit the team and dropped out of college. He spent the next year working odd jobs and trying to figure out what to make of his life. He spent a few months pumping gas in Hartford, Connecticut. Then he hopped a bus to Washington, D.C., and worked on a construction crew building the Pentagon in Arlington, Virginia. Eventually Kerouac decided to join the military to fight for his country in World War II. He enlisted in the U.S. Marines in 1943, but was honorably discharged after only 10 days of service for what his medical report described as "strong schizoid trends."

I do not know, I do not care and it does not make any difference.

- Jack Kerouac

After his discharge from the Marines, Kerouac returned to New York City and fell in with a group of friends that would eventually define a literary movement. He befriended Allen Ginsberg, a Columbia student, and William Burroughs, another college dropout and aspiring writer. Together, these three friends would go on to become the leaders of the Beat Generation of writers.

Living in New York in the late 1940s, Kerouac wrote his first novel, Town and City, a highly autobiographical tale about the intersection of small town family values and the excitement of city life. The novel was published in 1950 with the help of Ginsberg's Columbia professors, and although the well-reviewed book earned Kerouac a modicum of recognition, it did not make him famous.

'On the Road'

Another of Kerouac's New York friends in the late 1940s was Neal Cassady; the two took several cross-country road trips to Chicago, Los Angeles, Denver, and even Mexico City. These trips provided the inspiration for Kerouac's next and greatest novel, On the Road, a barely fictionalized account of

these road trips packed with sex, drugs and jazz. Kerouac's writing of On the Road in 1951 is the stuff of legend: He wrote the entire novel over one three-week bender of frenzied composition, on a single scroll of paper that was 120 feet long.

Like most legends, the story of the whirlwind composition of On the Road is part fact and part fiction. Kerouac did, in fact, write the novel on a single scroll in three weeks, but he had also spent several years making notes in preparation for this literary outburst. Kerouac termed this style of writing "spontaneous prose" and compared it to the improvisation of his beloved jazz musicians. Revision, he believed, was akin to lying and detracted from the ability of prose to capture the truth of a moment.

However, publishers dismissed Kerouac's single-scroll manuscript, and the novel remained unpublished for six years. When it was finally published in 1957, On the Road became an instant classic, bolstered by a review in The New York Times that proclaimed, "Just as, more than any other novel of the '20s, The Sun Also Rises came to be regarded as the testament of the 'Lost Generation,' so it seems certain that On the Road will come to be known as that of the 'Beat Generation'." As Kerouac's girlfriend at the time, Joyce Johnson, put it, "Jack went to bed obscure and woke up famous."

Later Works

In the six years that passed between the composition and publication of On the Road, Kerouac traveled extensively; experimented with Buddhism; and wrote many novels that went unpublished at the time. His next published novel, The Dharma Bums (1958), described Kerouac's clumsy steps toward

"My fault, my failure, is not in the passions I have, but in my lack of control of them."

\- Jack Kerouac

spiritual enlightenment on a mountain climb with friend Gary Snyder, a Zen poet. Dharma was followed that same year by the novel The Subterraneans, and in 1959, Kerouac published three novels: Dr. Sax, Mexico City Blues and Maggie Cassidy.

Kerouac's most famous later novels include Book of Dreams (1961), Big Sur (1962), Visions of Gerard (1963) and Vanity of Duluoz (1968). Kerouac also wrote poetry in his later years, composing mostly long-form free verse as well as his own version of the Japanese haiku form. Additionally, Kerouac released several albums of spoken word poetry during his lifetime.

Final Years

Despite maintaining a prolific pace of publishing and writing, Kerouac was never able to cope with the fame he achieved after On the Road, and his life soon devolved into a blur of drunkenness and drug addiction. He married Edie Parker in 1944, but their marriage ended in divorce after only a few months. In 1950, Kerouac married Joan Haverty, who gave birth to his only daughter, Jan Kerouac, but this second marriage also ended in divorce after less than a year. Kerouac married Stella Sampas, who was also from Lowell, in 1966. He died from an abdominal hemorrhage three years later, on October 21, 1969, at the age of 47, in St. Petersburg, Florida.

Legacy

More than four decades after his death, Jack Kerouac continues to capture the imagination of wayward and rebellious youth. One of the most enduring American novels of all time, On the Road appears on virtually every list of the 100 greatest American novels. Kerouac's words, spoken through the narrator Sal Paradise, continue to inspire today's youth with the power and clarity with which they inspired the youth of his own time: "The only people for me are the mad ones, the ones who are mad to live, mad to talk, mad to be saved, desirous of everything at the same time, the ones who never yawn or say a commonplace thing, but burn, burn, burn like fabulous yellow roman candles."

TRACKING JACK

The Beginning

"I see a vision of a great rucksack revolution, thousands or even millions of young Americans wandering around with rucksacks going up to mountains to pray, making children laugh and old men glad, making young girls happy and old girls happier, all of 'em Zen Lunatics who go about writing poems that happen to appear in their heads for no reason and also by being kind and also by strange unexpected acts keep giving visions of eternal freedom to everybody and to all living creatures."

- Jack Kerouac, the Dharma Bums

Jack, *Mad Jack, crazy man, King of the Zen Lunatics,*
Avatar of the Beats, father to the hippies,
lost wandering soul, where are you now?
On the Road, again?

The Ross Lake National Recreational Area is comprised of three lakes, created when the valley was damned and flooded to provide power to Seattle and northern Washington State. The aspiring pilgrim will drive alongside the mighty Skagit River from Bellingham and first pass by the new Gorge Dam, constructed in 1961. The dam is 300 feet high and produces 175,000 kilowatts of electric energy.

On the Road to Desolation Peak

The journey into the past that became the future begins in the present on the roaring hell of Interstate 5 - where semi-trailers jammed full of consumer products that people don't really need or actually want but waste their lives trying to acquire because they have no deeper spiritual ambitions other than owning a giant plasma high definition TV to watch soap operas about other people's lives or cheering on their favourite football team - belch their bellicose way between the mega-malls of the Pacific northwest.

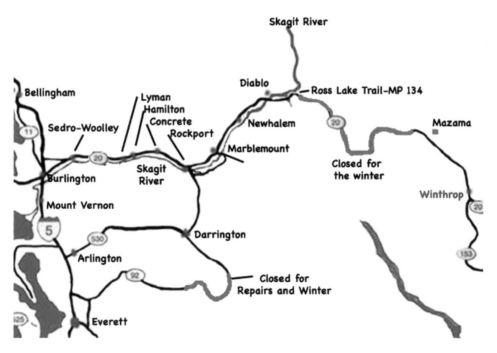

Diablo Dam

The dam was built in 1929 and a road was constructed on the top of the dam at that time to allow for maintenance. More recently the North Cascades Institute was built on the west shores of Diablo Lake. The only access to NCI is via the road over the Diablo dam. The waters of Diablo Lake are a dazzling aquamarine, and NCI allows guests to explore the lake via the Institute's giant canoe.

At Burlington, south of Bellingham, the spiritual pilgrim turns eastward onto rustic Highway 20, winding its bucolic way along the Skagit River valley through increasingly smaller towns like Concrete, Marblemount, and Newhalem. Then it's the tiny company village of Diablo, so small you'll miss it if you blink, and then finally arriving at the parking lot at a retreat called the North Cascades Institute built on the banks of emerald-green alpine-fed Diablo Lake, where a mighty dam churns out electricity for Seattle Light and Power and millions of its customers busy burning up the planet in a headlong rat race to nowhere.

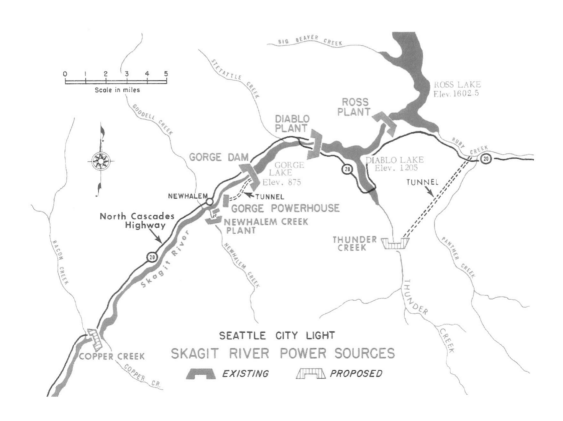

The Other Side of Diablo

The dam creates 159,000 kilowatts of power. Behind the dam the intrepid Kerouac pilgrim will find the tiny company town of Diablo, where the maintenance employees live. Also on this side of the dam can be found the funicular railroad that was used by Gary Snyder and Jack Kerouac in 1956 to be hoisted up from Diablo to a height equal to Diablo Lake.

When beat generation writer Jack Kerouac hitchhiked all the way up here from San Francisco in the middle 1950s, following on the heels of poet and environmental pioneer and friend Gary Snyder, this is where the road finally ended. Highway 20 went no further, defeated by the peaks of the mighty Cascades and the deepest winter snow on the planet. There was no NCI then, or much of anything other than trees and the jagged peaks of twisted and distorted mountains. Right smack up next to the Canadian border, this was as far away from mainstream middlebrow America as it was possible to run, lost in the deep Cascades Wilderness. Which is just what Mad Jack wanted, to see if peacefulness and serenity would do for his tortured soul what drugs and booze in New York and San Francisco apparently wouldn't.

The North Cascades Institute

A spectacular architect-designed campus, the North Cascades Institute offers an annual Poets on the Peaks literary excursion every August. Dormitory and single room accommodations are available in a beautiful building in a remote wooded setting.

I park in the lot at North Cascades Institute and wander around the grounds. NCI has been working in and around this region since 1986, their mission statement saying the college "helps connect people, nature and community through science, art, literature and the hands-on study of natural and cultural history." Their goal is to help people of all ages experience and enjoy the mountains, rivers, forests, people and wildlife of the Pacific Northwest so everyone will care for and protect this special place. Maybe if NCI had been around for Jack back then, it could have served as the sanatorium he truly needed.

NCI Offices and Classrooms

Aside from hosting the Poets on the Peaks excursion, NCI offers a wide range of outdoors activities, workshops, and environmental studies at its modern campus on the shores of Ross Lake.

Whatever their goal, they certainly have built a lovely retreat. In 2005, North Cascades Institute opened what they call the Environmental Learning Centre, which is the current campus. The tree-sheltered campus features 16 buildings on the north shore of Diablo Lake right underneath Sourdough Mountain where Gary's Snyder's own retreat is still found high atop the peak, a fire lookout just like Kerouac's own lookout across the valley at Desolation Peak.

Sourdough Mountain Lookout, Gary Snyder's L.O. in 1953 & Philip Whalen's in 1954 and '55

The fire lookout where Phillip Whalen and Gary Snyder worked from 1953-56 can be seen to the west from Ross Lake.

Diablo Lake

Paddling the big canoe is one of many activities available for family and friends to explore the beautiful alpine waters of Diablo lake.

Facilities at the campus include overnight lodging for up to 92 participants in three separate dormitories. There are multimedia classrooms, a library and meeting spaces. The lakeside dining hall serves up healthy vegetarian food. An outdoor amphitheater allows for performances and readings. Several outdoor learning shelters are scattered about in the woods. There are trails leading into the surrounding mountains and up to Ross Lake, and a dock on Diablo Lake for paddling adventures, mainly in NCI's giant canoe.

Ross Lake Dam

Ross Lake Dam stands high above Diablo Lake, holding back the waters of massive Ross Lake and generating power for the Pacific Northwest.

But I'm not here for vegetarian food, any more than Jack Kerouac was interested in granola and whole wheat when he came here in 1956. I'm here to find the spirit of Jack, whatever is left of it, high atop distant Desolation Peak. More than fifty years after his death, his writing remains as vital as ever, his books still in print, his words still inspiring millions of young people to rebel, to challenge the rules, to find some meaning of their own in their lives, to flee the rat race through wanderlust and exploration. Hit the road, Jack, and don't come back.

Ross Dam is a 540-foot (160 m)-high, 1,300-foot (400 m)-long concrete thin-arch dam across the Skagit River. t is a concrete thin-arch dam 540 feet (160 m) high and about 1,300 feet (400 m) long, stretching across one of the narrowest spots in the Skagit Gorge. The power plant of Ross Dam is located just downstream of its base and produces 460 MW of power from four hydroelectric turbines. The dam has two over-the-crest spillways on its flanks, each with six individual spillway bays.

I settle in to my room and then head down to the cafeteria for dinner. That night a bright white moon lights up a star-filled sky and I sit in my room and read a copy of Kerouac's The Dharma Bums, which describes his trip to this very spot. The next morning dawns cloudy, but I explore the lake via canoe and then catch a ride with NCI director Saul Weisberg, who agrees to take me in the Institute's powerboat across Diablo Lake to the foot of gigantic Ross Dam. We manage to get very close to the towering structure, dam security notwithstanding, and I attempt to imagine what it would feel like to ascend up the dam via a winch, as Kerouac did.

Saul Weisberg

Saul Weisberg, a naturalist, writer and ecologist, is the co-founder and executive director of the North Cascades Institute.

"To get to the starting point of the trail to Desolation Peak these days," says Saul, wrapped up in a jacket and hood in the chill morning breeze at the steering wheel of the boat, "you don't go up Diablo Lake any more. There's a tourist ferry that will run you up the lake to the foot of the dam, but the actual trailhead is found off the highway on the east side of Ross Lake. You'll get on a barge there, and a park ranger named Gerry Cook will take you up the lake on an old World War Two landing craft called The Mule."

Diablo Village

The tiny company village of Diablo is located south of the Diablo dam, along the shores of the Skagit River. There are no stores or other facilities in the village.

In order to arrive at their respective mountaintops in the mid-fifties, Snyder - who had ensconced himself a year earlier atop nearby Sourdough Peak to study Zen Buddhism, and Kerouac the following year on Desolation Peak above Ross Lake - had to ride a funicular railway up from Diablo village to the Diablo Dam. Then, for Kerouac to get to Desolation Peak, it was another barge ride across Diablo Lake to Ross Lake, then the barge hoisted up the side of the mighty dam in a winch, then an overnight stay aboard the barge, then another barge ride up Ross Lake, then a mule ride up the 6,000-foot slopes of appropriately titled Desolation Peak to finally arrive at the tiny fire lookout at the top. Quite the expedition. While the access to Ross Lake has gotten a bit easier these days, it's still a long journey.

High Above Ross Lake

The hills in the North Cascades Wilderness are very steep. Ross Lake is a drowned river valley, formed when the Seattle Light and Power Company built a dam and flooded the low-lying bottom lands.

But the real journey for the modern pilgrim curious to find what drew the Beat poets to these remote mountaintops really begins much further back than that. Today, cynics all of us, we laugh at the naïve "peace, love and happiness" hippie generation of the 1960s, but in truth the world derived much of its modern fervour for saving our great green beautiful planet from those silly hippies, and in truth the hippie generation borrowed much of its environmental ethics from Dharma Bums like Kerouac, who in fact borrowed many of those values from true outdoorsman Snyder, one of the world's first environmentalists.

Ross Lake Dam

Heavy winter snowfall and rain in the other months make for a wet climate. Glacial melt and heavy runoff fill the reservoirs to capacity most years.

That's when the "green revolution" really started, way back in the early 1950's, in the post-war blues when a young Gary Snyder rejected the mindless consumerism of the young American baby boomers so eager to buy a stucco bungalow in the suburbs and have 2.5 children and a black and white TV set and watch Ed Sullivan on Sunday nights after going to church on a Sunday morning in their shiny new Chevrolet, and set out to find for himself a lifestyle that had a deeper spiritual meaning than a cheap buggy in the garage and black folks still rode in the back of the bus and there were no gay people. This where a key part of the hippie "back to the land" revolution began, in Snyder's little wooden fire lookout high atop secluded Sourdough Mountain in the remote North Cascades Mountains of Washington State.

Gary Snyder, today.

Fire Lookouts: Places of Reflection and Inspiration

Ross Lake National Recreation Area
North Cascades National Park Service Complex

Seasons spent at fire lookouts in the North Cascades proved inspirational for Jack Kerouac, Gary Snyder, and Philip Whalen - poets and writers of "The Beat Era" - each of whom published books with rich imagery of this place.

"Two seasons on lookouts...gave me full opportunity to watch the change of mood over vast landscapes, light moving with the day - the countless clouds, the towering cumulus..." Gary Snyder -- *Mountains & Rivers Without End*

Poet-writer Jack Kerouac's spiritual quest and his desire for simplicity and solitude, led him to seek work as a fire watcher during the summer of 1956 at Desolation Lookout. The experience proved to be influential in his life, contributing much to *The Dharma Bums, Desolation Angels, Lonesome Traveler,* and *Book of Blues.*

"In the morning...I went out in my alpine yard and there it was, everything that Japhy (Gary Snyder) had said it was, hundreds of miles of pure snow-covered rocks and virgin lakes and high timber...on my 6,600 foot pinnacle. I...named all the magic rocks and clefts, names Japhy had sung to me so often...the circumstances of existence are pretty glorious."
Jack Kerouac -- *The Dharma Bums*

Jack Kerouac at Gary Snyder's going away party, May 1956 - six weeks before Jack's sixty-three day stay at Desolation Lookout.

Seen from Desolation Lookout, Hozomeen Mountain dominates the northern horizon. For Jack Kerouac, Hozomeen's essential solidness set amid constantly changing light and clouds was a symbol of inner tranquility.

"...look at Hozomeen, is he worried or tearful? Does he bend before storms or snarl when the sun shines or sigh in the late day drowse? Does he smile? Was he not born of madbrained turmoils and upheavals of raining fire and now's Hozomeen and nothing else? Why should I choose to be bitter or sweet, he does neither? Why can't I be like Hozomeen and...'take life as it comes'..." Jack Kerouac -- *Desolation Angels*

On the National Register of Historic Places and built by the U.S. Forest Service, Desolation Lookout (1932) and Sourdough Lookout (1933) continue to serve as fire lookouts now staffed by the National Park Service.

On a clear day you can see the twin spires of Hozomeen Mountain, and with binoculars Desolation Lookout may also be visible perched atop Desolation Peak.

Historic Lookout

On Highway 20 east of Diablo Lake, a signboard has been erected, naming this region of National Historic significance due to the writings of poets Phillip Whalen and Gary Snyder, and novelist Jack Kerouac, who spent summers atop the local mountains.

On Highway 20 just east of Ross Dam a signboard has been erected by the National Parks Service explaining and pointing the way to the fire lookouts atop Desolation Peak and Sourdough Mountain. The signboard sports a photo of Kerouac taken at Snyder's "going away party" just before Snyder left San Francisco to come to the Cascades, his second trip to the region, a trip that Kerouac would follow just six weeks later. The signboard explains that the fire lookouts were a "place of reflection and inspiration" that inspired the Beat poets like Snyder and Phillip Whalen. This news about "serenity" might have surprised the fire lookouts who came before Snyder and Kerouac, outdoorsmen who weren't poets and writers at all and wouldn't have understood or appreciated a Zen haiku if you spelled one out by syllables.

View from Historic Lookout

The lookout offers spectacular views up Ross Lake, all the way to the jagged peak of Mt. Hozamneen at the Canadian border.

The sign explains this exact location is named on the National Registry of Historic Places and it contains quotes from The Dharma Bums and Snyder's book of poetry Mountains and Rivers Without End. It's a place of pilgrimage for many, and there are several tourists taking photos of the sign, so I stop and do so myself. I wonder what Kerouac would have thought about being on the list of National Historic Places. Perhaps he would have sat by the sign with a bottle of cheap wine and got drunk.

Mt. Hozameen and Desolation Peak

Those with good binoculars, or a zoom or telescopic lens, can see the jagged peak of Hozameen to the left, and the more rounded top of Desolation Peak to the right. The tiny roof of the fire lookout atop Desolation Peak where Kerouac spent one summer can be seen atop Desolation by those with very sharp eyes.

In the distance it is quite possible with the naked eye to see the sharp jagged peak of Mt. Hozameen and, if you know exactly where to look, the softer and rounder shape of Desolation Peak. In the zoom lens of my Panasonic Lumix camera with its wonderful 24X scope I strain to see if a tiny dot I spot atop Desolation could be Kerouac's cabin. I learn later that it is. Ross Lake twists and turns below the mighty peaks, with nary a single boat in sight. There is virtually no way to get a boat on to the lake from this southern end. The descent from the highway is just too steep for any road or cars and boats. The northern end of Ross Lake touches just inside the Canadian border and Canadian paddlers do bring canoes and kayaks down the lake on occasion, but very few boats wander this far south.

Funicular Railway

The power house of the old funicular railway is now abandoned. It sits atop a very steep hill, down which the old rail cars used to run to Diablo Village. Access to this site is now restricted.

The next day, armed with a copy of The Dharma Bums and an excellent guide to the region titled Beats on the Peaks found in the NCI library I set forth on foot from the NCI campus to explore Diablo Dam. To access NCI on the western shore you need to drive the road built across the top of the dam. From atop the structure you can see all the way up Diablo Lake. Looking the other way, however, there is a deep canyon and a thin ribbon of old paved road heading south. My intention is to find where this particular road leads, and to see if the funicular railroad mentioned in the Kerouac and Snyder books is still standing.

Funicular Railway

Back in the 1950's, before Highway 20 was extended eastwards, the access to Ross Lake was via this funicular road. Rail cars used to be hoisted up this steep incline to a road at the top that leads to the Diablo Dam, from where boats can be taken to Ross Lake dam.

There is a railroad atop the dam and some sort of towing device is stowed at the far western end of the dam. This doesn't look like any type of winch that could be used to haul any equipment up the side of the dam, so I stride manfully down the road to see where the road will go. It's obviously in good repair, so I figure there must be some reason for it to be maintained. A few hundred yards down the road I note a small trail that heads to the left, also in good condition, meaning people are using it for some reason. I hike down the trail for a mile or so, and who so surprised as I to come around a corner and find myself directly above the little village of Diablo far below. It looks possible to descend down into the canyon on foot and I am tempted to do so, just to see if there is a store where I can ask some questions about the long lost funicular used by both writers to ascend to the lofty heights of the Diablo dam. But to hike down and return would take hours, so I give it a pass and return to the road.

Funicular Railway

During the author's visit, the railway was still in decent condition although no longer operating.

I walk no more than a few hundred yards more down the pavement and come around the corner and voila! My breath is taken away. There is a stop sign, a gate and some steps leading upward to a corrugated metal shack cut into the granite sides of Sourdough Mountain, and descending steeply from the shack are the ancient rails, wires and wheels of the funicular railway that I had assumed had been destroyed decades ago. Standing on the top of the rails, it looks quite a steep ride down to the bottom. The railroad is in serious disrepair, but I eventually learn that it was actually put to use a few years ago when Highway 20 was closed due to heavy snowfalls.

Far below is the tiny village of Diablo, a company town for employees of Seattle Light and Power. The village is not visible from Highway 20 and chances are very few people ever detour from the main road to discover this tiny jewel. I can see a few dozen houses, a giant water tower, power lines and a river running through the canyon. It looks a lovely little village and I am once again intrigued by the thought of knocking on doors and asking villagers about their knowledge of the railroad – and of Kerouac and Snyder, of course – but my suspicion is that nobody will ever have heard of the Beat Generation, or of either men. It's a long way back to 1956. I creep my way down the gravel to the bottom of the funicular and it's still a long way to the town. I try to imagine Kerouac riding the rails up this mountain; a far cry from the freight trains on which he once worked in his job as a brakeman.

Trail Down to Ross Lake

The trail down to the top of Ross Lake dam is found at the back of a small parking lot a few miles east of the village of Diablo. The very steep trail takes about 45 minutes to descend. Back country permits are required past this point.

The next day we Beats on the Peaks pilgrims are up bright and early, piling into three vans bound for the beginning of the trail that will eventually lead us to Desolation Peak. There are ten pilgrims in the hiking party, leader Gerry Cook and NCI staffer Jeff Muse leading eight followers on the trek. There are two Steve's, two Gerry's, two Holly's, one Diane and a Michael following a Cook and a Muse up the steep trail, most of us over fifty years old and all hailing from the northwest, and all Kerouac aficionados. The beat writer has been dead for 50 years and boasts far more readers now than when he was alive. Everyone on the hill is older than Kerouac when he rode a mule up the Desolation trail at the age of 34, but no one today is a heavy smoker or drinking themselves to death either.

Trail's End
The trail down to the lake ends at the top of Ross Lake dam.

The Ross Lake trailhead is nothing more than a small parking lot on the west side of the highway, perhaps a half mile east of the lake and high above the dam. Anglers heading for a small floating lodge near the dam park their vehicles way up here and hike down a very steep trail. It might be possible for two strong men to carry a canoe or kayak down the trail but I confess I am not the man to volunteer to do it. Supplies to the lodge come from Diablo Lake, where a small boat can start from near Diablo dam and dock just below the giant Ross Lake powerhouse. A truck runs back and forth from the dock by the powerhouse and up to the dam and then across the dam to a small marina, then by boat to the lodge.

There is a signboard at the top of the trail listing the rules and regulations pertaining to the backwoods park where we are headed. Reservations for camping sites are required and must be made well in advance. There are very few campsites available, and no services of any sort. Evidently there is a phone booth at the bottom of the trail where those people with reservations can call the fishing lodge to hail a water taxi. Otherwise you are completely on your own.

Ross Lake Dam

The Mule is an old World War Two landing craft, perfect for landing on a lake with no beaches. It is usually moored at the gatehouse seen at the top of the photo, at the dam on the very south end of Ross Lake.

Everybody in our party is carrying a fairly large pack. We need to tote our own tents, sleeping bags, food and clothing for all sorts of weather. It can rain heavily here in the North Cascades at any time, even in the middle of summer, and hikers are well advised to be ready for anything. I have no pack; I am carrying a duffel bag, slung over both shoulders, which is a tad awkward but I know it's only a mile down to the lake and then we will store our equipment aboard the boat. I estimate the bag weighs 30 to 40 pounds; the straps dig heavily into my shoulders, but it's only a 45-minute hike, and straight down, so no worries.

"I'd like everyone to follow me carefully and not stop or wander off," says Cook. "I'd like to get down to the bottom and find we are all there. There's a confusing choice of trails at the bottom and I don't want anyone to get lost. Stay right behind me."

The day is overcast, with thick clouds wafting down the lake from the north. It's quite cool, and though we all enjoy a good workout descending down the trail it's in good condition and I have no problem with my bag. As advertised, there are several roads down near the dam and it's confusing, but since I am last in the party - slow from taking lots of photos - I find everybody waiting patiently for me when I arrive. Down here, the dam is absolutely immense. Everybody takes time to peer over the edge down at the canyon several hundred feet below. Then Gerry musters the troops and gives everybody the drill about riding on his pride and joy, the ancient (World War Two, he says) landing craft he has named the Ross Lake Mule, a funky watercraft that has served loyally to ferry hikers and supplies up and down the lake for many years.

Ross Mule

The Ross Mule is an old World War Two landing craft, with a front loading deck that can be lowered to access a dock or shoreline. There are no beaches on Ross Lake. The cabin is only big enough for the skipper, and the deck is open, providing no shelter from wind or rain.

"There's life jackets for everyone," says Gerry, delivering his instructions by the side of the dock. "Pile your bags there by the side of the cabin. There's only enough room for one or two people inside the cabin, so keep your jackets ready in case of rain. It's pretty cold out on the water anyway so you'll need them."

There's a picnic table in the middle of the Mule, a few scattered chairs, and a storage box for life jackets and food, but everything else is out in the open. The front of the landing craft is what makes it unique. A loading gate rises up and down at the flick of a switch inside the cabin. There are no beaches anywhere on the lake, which was formed by flooding the steep Ross River Valley many decades ago. The landing craft lowers the front gate to allow supplies to be delivered to shore or a dock, and removed. It's a beauty.

Ross Lake Resort

Ross Lake Resort is a small floating community, the only accommodations on the lake, and very difficult to access. There are no roads, and most boats are forbidden.

The skies begin to lift as we pull out. Well away from the dam, the views both up and down the lake are spectacular. Ross Lake Lodge turns out to be a string of large floating cabins on the west side of the lake. There appears to be electricity for the cabins and small fishing boats are tied up in front of most cabins. This has to be one of the most difficult lodges to access in all of America, I think, as we drift by aboard the Mule. I love the fact that there are no jet skis, powerboats or other types of noisy watercraft on Ross, the type of junk that pollutes lakes all over America. The only sound is the soft chugging of the Mule's diesel engine as we plow our way up the lake. To the south the flat tabletop of Paul Bunyan's Peak dominates the view. Looking north to Canada, our direction, I see soft pale blue skies.

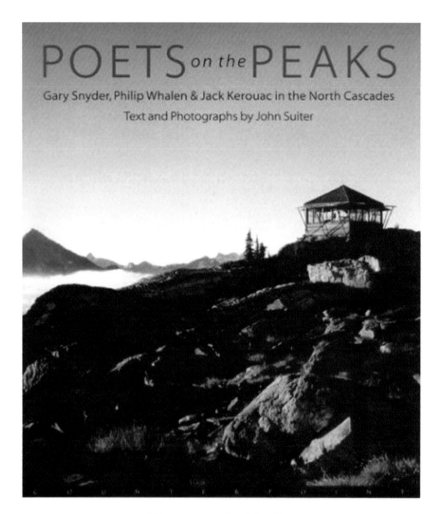

Poets on the Peaks

A beautifully illustrated book by writer John Suiter of Beat icons Jack Kerouac, Gary Snyder, and Philip Whalen and the years in the Cascades high country that shaped their lives and work. The book evolved from a magazine assignment that took Suiter to Jack Kerouac's remote fire lookout on Desolation Peak on the fortieth anniversary of the publication of The Dharma Bums for two weeks in the summer of 1995. http://www.poetsonthepeaks.com

We sit at the table and watch the world go by. It will be a few hours before we get to Lightning Creek, our campsite and destination for the night and starting point for the steep climb up Desolation Peak tomorrow. I sit down and dig out my Poets on the Peaks book and start to read.

"The only people for me are the mad ones, the ones who are mad to live, mad to talk, mad to be saved, desirous of everything at the same time, the ones who never yawn or say a commonplace thing, but burn, burn, burn, like fabulous yellow roman candles exploding like spiders across the stars and in the middle you see the blue center light pop and everybody goes Awww!" – Jack Kerouac

The movement really only flourished from the mid-1950s until the early 1960s. The most prominent members of the movement were the novelists John Clellon Holmes and Kerouac himself, along with poets Allen Ginsberg, Lawrence Ferlinghetti, Philip Whalen, Gary Snyder and Gregory Corso. Novelist William Burroughs was loosely associated with the Beat literary scene, whose members swung back and forth between America's two most open-minded communities, North Beach in San Francisco and Greenwich Village, New York City.

Literary historians have suggested that the Beat movement had two distinct phases, the "underground scene" from 1944 to 1956, when the Beats were traveling and writing, and then the public movement from 1956-62 when the beats began to be published and started to perform. Holmes is credited with introducing the term Beat Generation in a 1952 essay about his novel GO. Later on Kerouac attempted to explain that the term "beat" had several meanings. Beat meant being socially marginalized and exhausted (as in "beaten down") but also spiritually blessed (as in "beatific"). Many members of the Beats also were jazz enthusiasts, especially the bebop stylings, which gives a third meaning to the term. Much of Beat poetry was performance orientated, often read in public with jazz accompaniment.

William Burroughs, Allen Ginsberg & Jack Kerouac

The Beat Generation was really a short-lived phenomenon that had little immediate impact on America in the 1950's but obviously has had a long lasting influence ever since. A lot of Beat writing and poetry was published by Ferlinghetti's City Lights imprint, and his City Lights bookstore in North Beach was an important meeting-place for the group.

"Everything is going to the beat," wrote Kerouac. "It's the beat generation, it's be-at, it's the beat to keep, it's the beat of the heart, it's being beat and down in the world and like old time lowdown and like in ancient civilizations the slave boatmen rowing galleys to a beat and servants spinning pottery to a beat..."

In a post-World War Two America, the country exhausted from years of strife and the horror of war and striving for "normalcy," social pressure was applied on most people to follow a straight and narrow path, but the Beats grew weary of the conformity and extolled individual freedom and attacked what they saw as the materialism, militarism, consumerism, and conformity of the 1950s. In his classic 1957 novel On the Road, Kerouac wrote: "America, where everyone is always doing what they ought."

Unlike James Dean, the Beats were rebels with a cause. They affected non-conformist styles of dress and speech and, avowedly anti-materialist, they cultivated mystical experiences by the use of drugs or by meditation. There was a lot of dope smoking and drinking of wine and experiments with some psychedelics like peyote. Starting with Snyder and Phillip Whalen, a lot of Beats developed an interest in different forms of eastern mysticism and Zen Buddhism in particular.

The Beats were politically radical, avowedly left, I read on, which caused a great deal of antipathy towards the movement among American politicians and authority figures. To some degree their anti-authoritarian attitudes were taken up by political activists in the later 1960s. Popular social columnist Herb Caen in the San Francisco Chronicle derided them as communists and labelled them as "beatniks," a reference to the early Soviet spacecraft called Sputnik.

The Mule on Ross Lake

Ross Lake is 24 miles long, and the Mule is one of the very few watercraft allowed on its waters.

Although they were parodied and satirized in print and on TV, the Beats brought fresh energies to American writing and their social influence can obviously be seen as significant. The development of the "back to the land" hippie movement in the mid to late 1960's overtook the Beats and their bebop literary style soon faded away, but over time they have become viewed as America's first "anti-establishment" radicals. I put the book down and look around at the scenery. Gorgeous. Is this where it all began, the modern world and the environmental movement, on the mountains with Snyder's Zen haikus?

The Mule has been carrying passengers and cargo up and down Ross Lake as long as Captain Gerry Cook can remember. Gerry is now a park superintendent but prior to that he was a park ranger and before that he spent two summers as a fire lookout himself atop Desolation Peak in the early 1970s, following closely in the footsteps of Kerouac. Since then Gerry has made many treks to the top of Desolation, leading literary groups such as NCI's annual Beats on the Peaks hike and Kerouac fans such as ours. At the wheel inside the cabin, he explains that more, not fewer, people are making the pilgrimage to the top of the mountain as the years go by and the word gets out there is a Kerouac destination to which the intrepid follower can trace the mad man's steps.

"When he died, back in1969, he was a pretty obscure figure," says Cook, keeping an eye on the horizon while looking up at Desolation. "It was the hippie generation by then, and Kerouac had become something of an embarrassment, I think. He literally drank himself to death. There wasn't anybody making any treks up here then to see where he wrote. That sort of thing didn't happen until way later."

Secret Side Passage
The Mule, under the guidance of skipper Gerry Cook, makes its way into a secret side cove on the east side of Ross Lake.

Kerouac was more than an embarrassment by the time he died. He acted the fool. He appeared dead drunk on TV shows, making an ass of himself. His books did not sell well, and by the time he reached his personal expiry date he was completely broke, living off his mother at her little home in Florida, with only a few dollars in the bank. His books have since sold tens of millions of copies and are still in print today. He is studied in universities. Jack wouldn't have given a shit. He hated the hippies and literary critics.

The Mule is Cook's baby and he knows her well. He also knows Ross Lake like the back of his hand. The lake is full of little nooks and crannies, and Cook takes the time to ease the craft into several of them. There are hidden waterfalls in two small inlets. We pass under a bridge and into a side channel and Cook slowly navigates the Mule deeper and deeper into the channel. We pass a pair of kayakers investigating this magical little inlet themselves. The cries of birds echo back and forth between the granite walls, the only sounds to be heard aside from the low hum of the Mule's engines. Everyone is entranced, sitting quietly and saying nothing. This is a Snyder moment, not Mad Jack's.

Lightning Creek Camp

While there are no human services in the national park, the camp services that are provided are excellent. Lightning Creek Camp has a modern floating dock, storage and cooking facilities, a washroom and two picnic tables for the ten hikers in our party.

Finally, as the light begins to fade, we arrive at our overnight destination, the Lightning Creek Camp. There is a new wide wooden floating dock with a picnic table and shelter and a metal ladder that acts as a bridge to shore that we slide into place. Nearby hides a tidy campground in the woods, the perfect place to spend the night before setting forth in the morning to climb the mountain.

A deer grazes nonchalantly as we disembark and doesn't run. She watches me carefully as I set up my tent, the little shark-shaped beauty that was my home for a month when I trekked over the Himalayas from Nepal to the Tibetan plateau on a 500-mile trek inspired by the writings of Peter Matthiessen and his masterpiece The Snow Leopard. I approach quietly, wondering how close I can get before the creature bolts. I manage to get within ten feet before she turns and heads off slowly into the woods, turning back to look at me quietly. An enchanted moment.

Lightning Creek Camp

The cooking facilities at Lightning Creek are under cover, but if it starts to rain while you are dining, you will get wet.

Gerry has carried supplies of drinking water and fuel aboard the Mule. There is a camp stove at the shelter on the dock. He fires it up and one by one we cook our freeze-dried meals, chili and beans, whatever we have carried with us. Tea is brewed and we swap stories. The suns sets over Sourdough Mountain to the west. We sit and chat around the table as darkness slowly creeps over the hills and down the lake. This far north in the middle of summer it won't be fully dark until late in the evening. Finally we call it a night and crawl into our tents. Tomorrow will be a long day. We must ascend up to the peak at 6,085 feet where Kerouac's cabin rests like a tiny jewel on the crown, and then back down again all in one day, a vertical gain and drop of some 12,000 feet. That may take as many as 11 hours. I pull out my book again and read more about Poets on the Peaks by flashlight.

Paul Bunyan's Peak

Looking south on Ross Lake the bizarre shape of a mountain called Paul Bunyan's Stump can be seen, looking as if someone had taken an axe and cut off the top.

It's impossible to put a finger on any date when modern literature began, or when the "old days" ended and the new world began. Some say the end of the war in 1945, the emergence of the massive baby boomer generation that would change the world in so many ways. I allow myself the vanity of picking Wednesday, September 5, 1957, the date of my lucky seventh birthday and the day when the New York Times suddenly published a review of Kerouac's soon-to-be classic book On the Road.

Kerouac was 35. He had just descended from his retreat on top on Desolation Peak and re-entered the modern world to the hustle and bustle of New York City. The reviewer, Gilbert Millstein, called On the Road "the most beautifully executed, the clearest and the most important utterance yet made by the generation Kerouac himself named years ago as 'beat' and whose principal avatar he is."

Joyce Johnson, who wrote a memoir of her life among the Beat writers, was with Kerouac on that fateful day in New York when he picked up a copy of the paper at a news stand and read the extended rave review. She had gone with Kerouac to buy an early edition of the newspaper from an all-night stand in midtown Manhattan. In a nearby bar, she sat and watched him read and re-read Millstein's article, shaking his head "as if he couldn't figure out why he wasn't happier than he was." The fame that Kerouac had chased for years had finally arrived and it dawned on him that wasn't what he really wanted after all. One of the most famous literary reviews of all time actually depressed him. Go figure.

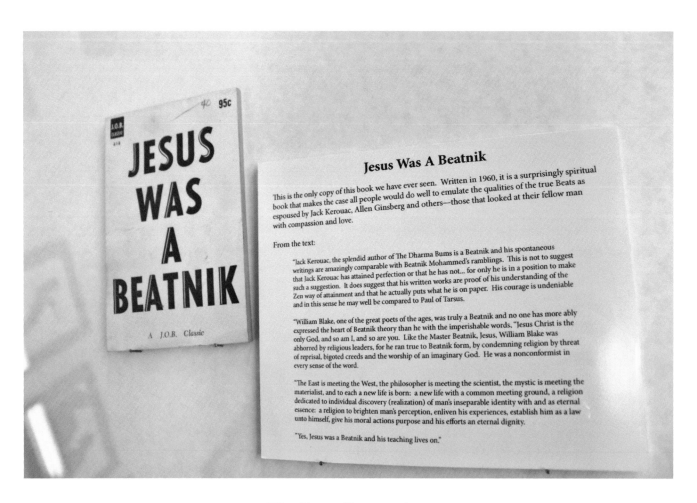

The Beat Generation

The word "Beatnik" was invented by Herb Caen, the gossip columnist for the San Francisco Chronicle. The word was inspired, he word, by the Russian word Sputnik (for space capsule) because he considered - as did much of mainstream media of the fifties - the Beats were really socialists to be vilified.

Afterwards they walked back to Johnson's apartment on the Upper West Side where Kerouac woke up the next morning to find out that he had become famous literally overnight. The Beat generation had finally become publically accepted, and Kerouac was being called the "avatar" of that movement. The review of On the Road would change his life and the reputation of being the Beat's leader would stay with him for the short period he lived afterwards, the reviewer's words haunting him forever. The book was heralded as "bringing a change of consciousness to the country" and based on that one New York Times review On the Road became a bestseller. It's still for sale in most bookstores in North America over 70 years after its initial publication.

More importantly, Kerouac's personal Beat look of blue jeans and t-shirt and boots, and his "I don't give a shit what the authorities have to say" demeanor changed the world in a way that few writers have ever done. As Kerouac's friend and fellow Beat writer William Burroughs sarcastically wrote later, the book also "sold a trillion Levi's, a million espresso coffee machines, and also sent countless kids on the road." As Kerouac was to find out to his great dismay, he had written a bible that would help determine the course of what would come to be known as "youth culture" over the following two decades. Any normal writer would have considered such a review in the New York Times as one of the greatest literary accomplishments possible. For Kerouac, it was depressing.

The Trail to Desolation Peak
The trail to Desolation Peak starts steep and stays steep for the next six hours.
It's just as steep on the way down too.

The next morning we pilgrims are all up early, take down our tents and pack up our gear, and stroll over to the dock for a quick breakfast of coffee and cereal. We are on the trail by 8 a.m. Immediately the trail, a narrow path wide enough only for one person, plunges into the deep woods and any view of the lake is lost. The trail starts steeply and stays steep the entire way. Gerry is at the front of the long line and keeps up a quick pace, a very quick stride for a man in his sixties. Chatter is kept to a minimum and we all have our thoughts to ourselves. While we walk a song rolls through my head in an endless loop, what I had been listening to the night before on my iPod, Bob Dylan's *Like a Rolling Stone.*

How does it feel
To be on your own
Like a rolling stone
Like a complete unknown
With no direction home?

The song was released in the middle 1960's, several years after *On the Road* was published. I was just ending high school at the time, and wondering about college. The song was a huge hit on the radio. You could hear it blasting out of car speakers, in bars and cafes, on the college campuses. It was an anthem, a call for change, a challenge to all who heard it. But while most listeners paid attention to the lyrics and sang along, I took the song to heart. I read *On the Road* at about the same time, and immediately put out my thumb and started to hitchhike. While others sang the song, I personally lived it.

Rocks Stars Influenced by Beats
Bob Dylan, The Doors, The Beatles and other rock bands

"It changed my life like it changed everyone else's," Bob Dylan would say many years later. Tom Waits, too, acknowledged its influence, calling the Beats "father figures." The book started what would later become the "road trip" genre, still being copied in film and literature to this day.

The legend goes that Kerouac originally wrote the On the Road manuscript back in 1951, taking three weeks and 120 feet of teletype paper to do so, fueled by strong coffee and reportedly lots of Benzedrine too. The entire book is one long road trip between New York and San Francisco and back, with a side trip to Mexico for fun. Kerouac carried the manuscript with him for years in an attempt to sell it to a publisher. No editor would touch it. "That's not writing, that's typing," said journalist Truman Capote of its strange jazz bebop style. Nobody understood it.

Meantime hipsters Elvis Presley, James Dean and Marlon Brando appeared on the scene. "The Beat literary movement came at exactly the right time," William Burroughs wrote, "and said something that millions of people all over the world were waiting to hear. The alienation, the restlessness, the dissatisfaction were already there waiting when Kerouac pointed out the road."

Though undoubtedly ambitious, Kerouac was utterly unprepared for the fame, notoriety and controversy that followed On the Road. He was hurt by the many negative reviews of the book, and by the parodies of the Beat generation that suddenly started appearing on mainstream television chat shows. In the end, he was just so depressed about how he was being misrepresented, how his great and beautiful book was being blamed for all the excesses of the Sixties.

Views of Ross Lake

The trail stays in deep forest nearly the entire way to the top of Desolation Peak, with views of the lake only emerging from time to time.

Had Kerouac not drank himself to death, he would have been even more appalled at the ways in which his legacy is currently being misrepresented. A few years ago a clothing retailer launched a Jack Kerouac clothing line. At the Naropa University in Boulder, Colorado, the Jack Kerouac School of Disembodied Poetics celebrated the 50th anniversary of On the Road with a three-day Kerouac festival. The last remnants of the Beat generation, or at least those fit enough to travel, were in attendance. One of the organizers, Junior Burke, described On the Road as "one of the truly defining works of American fiction, something that young people still relate to."

For most people in America, though, these days the name Jack Kerouac means nothing at all. Youth culture is increasingly defined by consumerism, which Kerouac would have despised. His generation's road trip has been replaced by the gap year. These days it's considered radical to be cool but not cool to be a radical. The great adventure that was travelling overland in the Sixties and Seventies has been replaced by a spring break party in Cancun. The notion that you would throw yourself at the mercy of the road, and gain some self-knowledge or even maturity, is long gone.

When I was a kid, I think as I trudge endlessly up Desolation Peak, On the Road instilled in me a belief that, in order to find oneself, one had to throw caution to the wind and travel long distances with no real goal and very little money. The instant I read the book I stuck out my thumb. I rode greyhounds across North America when I had enough money for the bus. I slept in hostels and in farmer's fields and in churches. I sang for my supper in Salvation Army choirs and panhandled on the street. I hopped freight trains. I have no idea what I was looking for, but I searched hard. One thing I knew, I didn't want a clerk's job and a stucco house in the suburbs and 2.5 kids and to vote for Richard Nixon and watch Dobie Gillis play bongo drums.

End of the Trail

Near the end of the trail the trees finally thin out, and reveal gorgeous views of Ross Lake far below.

There was no denying that the lives the Beats lived was edgy in a way that few generations are. They were transgressing the rules in a very real way and doing dangerous things at a time when such risks were high. Their lives were often more interesting than the books they were writing. As an aspiring writer, I wanted to follow the same path as my heroes. Kerouac, though, would probably hated having such things as "fans." I'm sure he didn't sign autographs.

We stop half way up the mountain, in a small clearing where we can see glimpses of the lake. We all have water bottles. No one has the breath to talk, so we sit and look at the lake. The clouds have cleared enough to see across and down the lake. We are in the proverbial 'middle of nowhere' and one wonders what Kerouac must have been thinking when he came up here riding a mule in a snowstorm in 1956. Tonight we will descend and return to the real world. Kerouac was going to spend 100 days on his own, facing his own demons, withdrawing from cigarettes and booze. In fact, he made the trek down the mountain a few days after to pick up some rolling tobacco he phoned down and ordered. He could do without the booze, but not his smokes.

William Burroughs, who was older and colder than the other Beats and perhaps envious of Kerouac's success, saw the Beat Generation as "a media construct with a shared transgressive vision. Those arch-opportunists," he wrote, "they know a story when they see one, and the Beat movement was a story, and a big one." Kerouac became the center of that story, constantly referred to in the media as king of the Beats and spokesman for a generation. He was eager for some kind of literary recognition, but certainly not suited candidate for the sainthood thrust upon him. Bob Dylan came along a decade later and managed to reinvent himself continually. Kerouac tried to adapt to changing times in the 60's and failed utterly.

The Lookout

After six hours of steep climbing, the famous fire lookout where Kerouac spent his most important summer finally comes into view, looking a lot like one of the Zen Buddhist poems that enchanted fellow fire lookout and poet Gary Snyder.

At about 5,000 feet we are stuck in the clouds, working hard, heads down, panting, pushing for the top. Nobody talks. Every few seconds I stop briefly and look up, hoping to see the peak so I can snap a photo of it. I've waited a long time and come a long way for this magic moment. Suddenly there is a shift in the clouds. The sky is pure white and the pine trees a blanket of green, then the clouds momentarily part and I get a glimpse. It's a Snyder haiku moment, like a Japanese screen painting. There, over 1,000 feet straight above, stands the tiny triangle-shaped roof of the hut, its angular lines in sharp contrast to the natural sculpture of rock and trees on which it sits.

It is so tiny (I learn later the cabin is only 14-feet square) the lookout seems completely lost in this vast wilderness, and I feel very small myself. Quickly I snap a photo and then the clouds close in and the image disappears as if I never saw it at all. I lower my head and keep walking and I wonder when we reach the apparition if will we be welcomed by the ghost of the mad man himself, for surely this is heaven and a place where his soul must have flown after emerging from the sad and tragic expiration of his mortal body in the pathetic environs of the sandy old folks graveyard that is the bleary Florida beach.

Kerouac died in 1969 in St Petersburg, alone and destitute. According to his close friends, the real Kerouac was essentially conservative, patriotic even, and old-fashioned in many ways. For instance, no one ever heard him swear. Yes, he was restless and questing, but also reserved and responsible. His intention was not freedom without responsibility, but his freedom of expression in art.

Elevation 6085

A wooden sign held in place by some rocks reveals the exact elevation as 6085 feet. Constant winds have weathered the paint on the front of the cabin. The cabin sits on concrete blocks, although the blocks that serve as the front steps are stored under the cabin on this day.

About 1,000 feet below the cabin the pine trees begin to thin out. The trail opens out onto grass and rock. We approach from the south. This close, I can't believe how small the cabin really is. It's tiny. It's mostly a faded white on the front, with some badly faded red trim. A wooden marker held in place by a large rock about 30 feet in front of the cabin greets visitors with a sign saying 6085 feet. The entire structure looks very frail, and I can't imagine what it must have been like to be inside it during a storm

There are windows on all sides, of course, to keep an eye on fires, but two sides today have wooden shutters on them, closing the cabin in. Two propane tanks lean against one wall, for the cabin is still active as a fire lookout although today the lookout is not here. A stovepipe sticks out the roof, which is comprised of asphalt black shingles.

Inside the Cabin

Inside the cabin, it's dark on this day and space is cramped for 10 people. The device Kerouac used to spot fires is still in place, stripped today of its map and pointer but still functional. Kerouac's bed and writing table are still in evidence

The cabin sits on concrete blocks, looking for all the world like it may blow away in a stiff wind. For some reason, the front steps are missing; there is one concrete block on which visitors can step to get inside. The front of the cabin – the side with the door - faces southeast, and the front door is closed with a heavy lock, but Gerry has the key. The cabin is raised up a couple of feet, and there are many concrete blocks stored under the floor, proof that the cabin is under repair.

Inside, the cabin is painted a light green colour and is indeed under repair, for furniture has been shoved over to one side, but there is Jack's bed and his writing table and a device that looks like a steering wheel but functions as a spotting device or would if the map and pointer were not missing. We crowd inside and take seats. As a party of ten, we take up most of the space. Time is tight, as we have to spend another 5-6 hours descending in order to get back to camp before dark. We chat about Jack. His spirit is tangible. He is in the room with us. We can feel it.

The Author Sits on Jack's Steps

The author takes a moment to rest his feet, and to sit in the exact spot where Mad Jack must have sat every morning enjoying the stupendous view. Note that the door is locked.

"You wouldn't believe what people who come here actually get up to," says Gerry. "If you read The Dharma Bums, it explains the daily routine that Jack kept. One paragraph mentions his standing upside down, so there was this French kid who came here just to do that. He stood on his head and looked at the world upside down, because it was written in the book. Then he left."

For myself, I feel compelled to sit in the doorway. Kerouac mentions that he did so every morning, so I do it too. I have spent lots of time alone on mountains over the years, but never 100 days by myself on a mountaintop as remote as this. I can't imagine what it would have been like for a drinker and party hound like Kerouac, deprived of his booze and friends and jazz, to be all alone in the silence. But today a light wind is blowing and the whisper of the words of Mad Jack floats through the air.

Looking Out the Front Door

Looking out the front door, the view is south towards Ross Lake, a fine sight for Kerouac to see every morning before breakfast.

"Oh, yes, it's quite something being up here in a storm," says Gerry, "especially when there is thunder and lightning. You have to stand on this rubber pad over here in case the cabin gets a direct hit so you don't get electrocuted. I spent a few hours on that pad one day, my hair standing straight up. Oh yes, she blows up here all right. She blows."

The clouds move in and out, allowing glimpses of the lake, Mount Hozzameen, and Soughdough in the distance. Even in a light wind, the cabin vibrates. I imagine Kerouac here, at night for 100 days, in the dark, alone with his demons. It's cold. I shiver.

Home at Last

Two propane tanks, presumably delivered by helicopter, lean against the side of the building, removing the need to chop down trees for firewood.

There is not enough room for all of us in the cabin for lunch so we go outside as the clouds clear momentarily and enjoy our sandwiches on the rocks with a fabulous view of the huge lake a mile below. You can almost see distant Sourdough Mountain on the west side of the lake from here, where Snyder spent his summers chopping wood and writing poetry. I spied it with my zoom lens earlier on the lake. Sinister, looming, jagged Mt. Hozamen to the north is not visible today because of thick clouds. Kerouac mentions its dark brooding presence in the Dharma Bums. Desolation Peak is well named. One can only imagine the sense of isolation during a storm, and I don't even want to think of it during thunder and lightning.

Picnic Lunch

The intrepid Kerouac fans from the Beats on the Peaks annual trek enjoy the view of Ross Lake by sitting outside the cabin where Kerouac may have eaten his own lunches.

Lunch over, it is time to leave, a long and winding road back to the madding world of cars and supermarkets and smart phones and mindless human chatter. It's a 10-12 hour slog to get up here and back, so very little time to spend with Jack, but his soul is here, drifting in the endless winds and sitting on the stoop, looking down on America. We start down the path and in a minute I turn around for one last look. "Sometimes I feel like a motherless child," goes the old blues refrain, and this is one of those times and places to feel that way. I turn again, head down the trail, and the moment is over like it never existed.

Homeward Bound

Somewhere down at the bottom of the 6,000-foot descent lies Lightning Camp, with the Mule tied up at the dock and ready to make the homeward cruise.

Which begs the inevitable question, does On the Road as a book stand the test of time? Is it a great work of literature? Some critics think so, comparing it to classics like Huckleberry Finn and The Great Gatsby, as a novel that 'explores the themes of personal freedom and challenges the promise of the American dream'. American novelist AM Homes wrote that 'Kerouac was the man who allowed writers to enter the world of flow... his philosophy was about being in the current, open to possibility, allowing creativity to move through you, and you to be one with the process'. Other critics disagree. The whole heart-on-the-sleeve romanticism of the book is off-putting, some say, even embarrassing. Apart from some really brilliant descriptive passages, it just does not stand up. It's become a different book now, a historical artefact rather than a living, breathing work of literature.

Journey's End

Kerouac's body lies buried in a cemetery in his home town of Lowell, Massachusetts. Notice the bottle of tequila a fan has placed on the gravestone. One of Kerouac's quotes, which might be defined as his philosophy of life, was this: "In the end, you won't remember the time you spent working in the office or mowing your lawn. Climb that goddam mountain." Desolation was Kerouac's mountain, and his end as well.

Assessing Kerouac and his impact on American culture by criticizing his writing style or how well On the Road stands up as a work of modern literature, however, seems to be missing the entire point of the man's life and philosophy. How does it fell to be on your own, with no direction home, like a complete unknown, like a rolling stone? Maybe only Mad Jack really knows, and apparently he ain't tellin.' If you want to find out for yourself, it's simple. You have to hit the road yourself. Start at Highway 20, head east and keep going.

Getting to Desolation Peak

Directions

Kerouac's cabin atop Desolation Peak is a very difficult destination to reach and requires serious advance planning. No one is allowed to camp at the fire lookout cabin on top of the mountain. Serious thought needs to be given as to where to stay overnight on your way to the top of the mountain and back. There are several options to get to the cabin, all of them difficult.

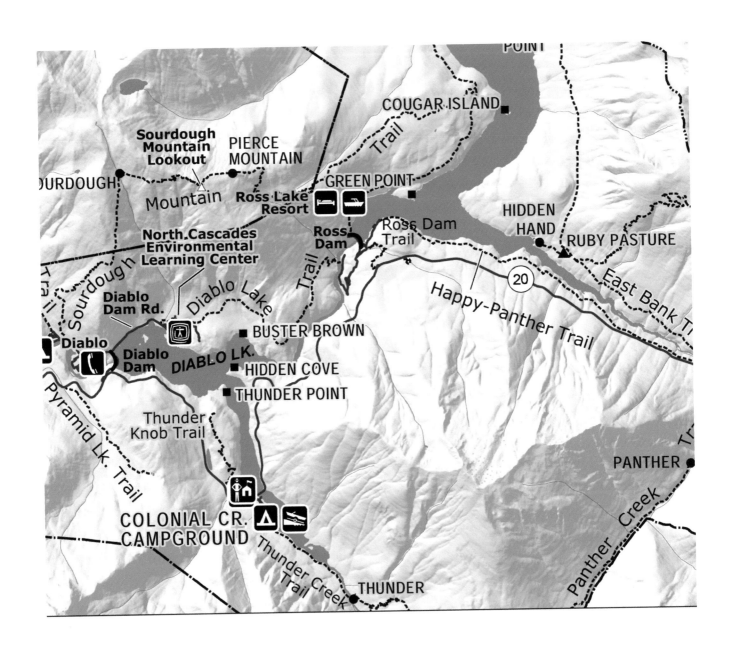

Option #1

The simplest option is to drive to Ross Lake by car, descend on foot by a marked trail from the parking lot on Highway 20 a few miles east of the village of Diablo, and proceed north on Ross Lake by a water taxi. Make a reservation with Ross Lake Resort well in advance, then call the Lodge from the phone (dial 18-31974) found on the last power pole by the side of the road at the bottom of the trail.

It's $2.00 per person for a quick boat ride across the lake to the resort, but that's only for people staying in the cabins or renting boats. Rates for water taxis to various campsites are included at the end of the book.

North Cascades Institute

Option #2

A second option is to sign up for the North Cascades Institute's annual Poets on the Peaks excursion described in this book, in mid-August, using the Mule landing craft that plies Ross Lake, but there are only 10 spots available. This expedition includes storytelling, an overnight campout at Lightning Creek, and fraternizing with fellow Kerouac fans. This is the best way to go. Plan well ahead.

Cascadian Ferry

Option #3

A third option is to drive to Diablo Lake, park at the Cascadian ferry dock, unload your own canoe or kayak, paddle 5 miles to the bottom of Ross Dam, and call for a portage to lift you around the dam on a truck owned by Ross Lake Lodge.

East Lake Trail

Option #4

A fourth option is to park off Highway 20 a few miles past the Ross Dam parking lot, and follow the East Bank trail about 16 miles (5 hours) to Lightning Camp, and stay there overnight. Lightning Camp camping details are at the end of the book.

Diablo Lake Ferries

Diablo Lake

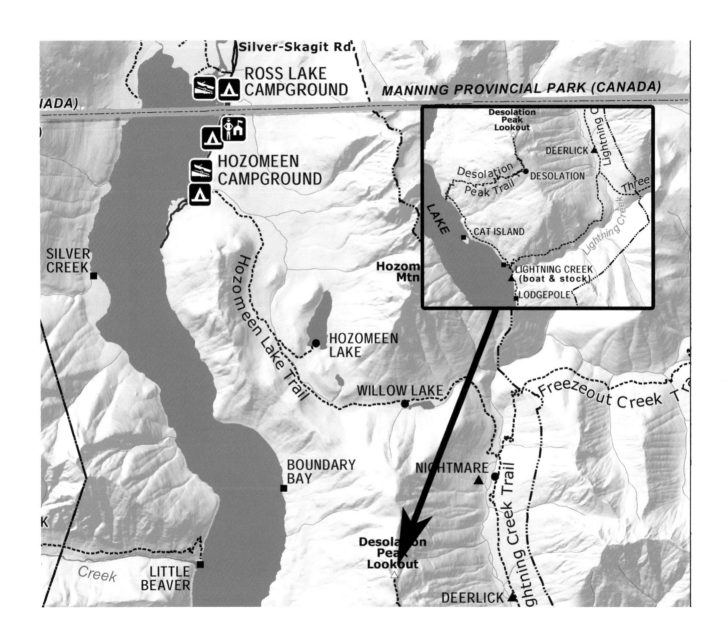

Lastly, it is possible to steer a 4-wheel drive vehicle down a rough road in Manning Provincial Park in British Columbia at the north end of Ross Lake in Canada, carrying a small craft on your vehicle, and then paddle or motor south down the lake to Lightning Camp. There is a provincial campsite at the lake. There are very few motor craft ever seen on the lake. Camping permits are required for everyone. Estimates of paddling times are your own, but it is wise to start early in the day.

Ross Lake, seen from the south end.

If you are not a Pacific Northwest local resident, schedule at least a week to get to Ross Lake and then back to your local accommodations in Seattle or elsewhere, whether starting from your home base in North America or in Europe. Make all reservations well in advance. The North Cascades is a region of very high precipitation and most years you can expect a lot of snowfall, so expect to wait until July to make an ascent to Desolation Peak. The Ross Lake region closes to any hiking at the end of October. At this elevation, you can expect rain, wind and cold weather any time during the summer months. Bring warm and waterproof clothing.

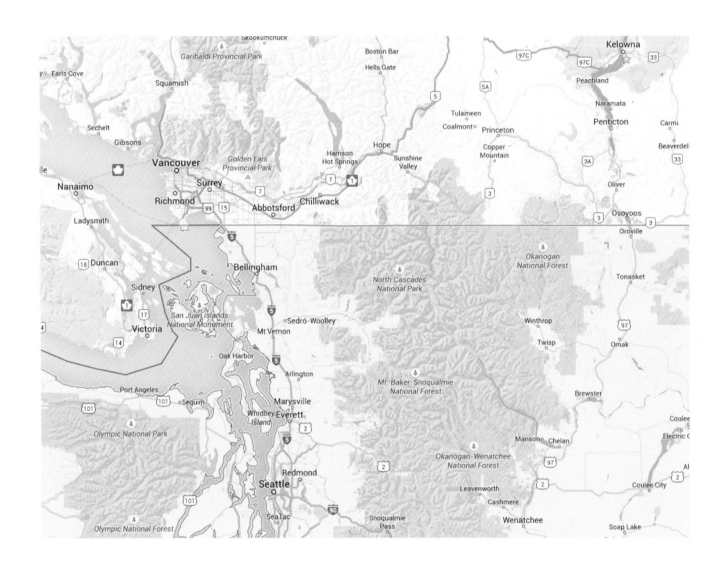

Arriving from overseas, there are major airports located at SeaTac Airport (located halfway between Seattle and Tacoma) and in Vancouver, British Columbia. From within the United States, some flights will take you at a lower fee to regional Bellingham Airport. From Vancouver airport (YVR) it is 189 kilometres, or 2 ½ hours driving time, to Ross Lake. The time spent crossing the border is not included in this estimate. It is the same distance and amount of driving time from SeaTac airport, but with no borders to cross.

Option #1

Ross Lake Resort

To drive to the Ross Lake Resort from Highway I-5 whether from north or south, turn off at Burlington and drive east on Highway 20 for 65 miles, and turn left on Diablo Dam Road between milepost 127 and 128. Cross Diablo Dam, turn right and park nearby at the Ross Lake Resort parking lot. Board the boat that departs at 8:30 a.m. and 3:00 p.m. daily and takes passengers to the end of Diablo Lake. Ross Lake Lodge has a truck parked there that takes passengers around the high dam and up to Ross Lake, where their boat (water taxi) is berthed. It is a very good idea to make a reservation with the Lodge water no roads leading down to it. Ross Lake was created by the damming of the Skagit River and is in the recreation area of the North Cascades National Park. The elevation of the to the cabin, each way. Ross Lake is a man-made reservoir in a steep valley and there are taxi well in advance. The fee from Ross Lake Lodge to portage a canoe or kayak is $30 per vessel, or $20 each for two or more.

Ross Lake Resort

Once you finally get to Lightning Camp, the only access to the peak itself is via a steep trail up from the camp, situated on the east shore of Ross Lake. It's about a 5-6 hour hike lake is 1600 feet and it is over 20 miles long.

The easiest access to Ross Lake is by foot, from a parking lot on Highway 20 a few kilometres east of the village of Diablo, at the south end of the lake, descending a steep trail on which you must carry your own food and camping supplies. There are about a dozen boat and foot campsites scattered around Ross Lake but all are very limited (1-7) in the number of tents allowed per site. The tent sites feature picnic tables, cooking grills and outhouses.

It might be possible for two people to carry a lightweight kayak down the hill from the Highway 20 parking lot, a 45-minute descent, but it would very difficult. An inflatable kayak might be possible, depending on the amount of weight you can carry on your back. Canoes or boats of any type would be impossible to carry down the trail.

When you arrive at Ross Lake, there is no immediate accommodation available aside from floating cabins at the Lodge. If you are camping, you will need to paddle north up the lake to your campground. Motorboats are available for hire.

Option #2

North Cascades Institute

The best way to enjoy a trek to Desolation Peak is to make the North Cascades Institute at Diablo Lake your home base, before and after the actual hike. If you plan well in advance, then you can simply join their annual Poets on the Peaks expedition in mid-

North Cascades Institute

August. This program includes 1 night lodging, 4 meals (dinner day 1, breakfast & sack use of an upper bunk, accessible by an easy-to-climb ladder). Double Accommodations is sharing a room with one other person. Single Accommodations is a room for one person.

The Learning Center campus features classrooms, a dining hall, a library, outdoor learning shelters, trails, a canoe dock and an amphitheater. Three guest lodges share gender-specific bathrooms with showers. Each room contains two sets of twin bunk beds, desks, wardrobes and wireless Internet connectivity. Facilities and local trails are all ADA accessible and a personal mobility vehicle is available. Delicious, healthy meals incorporating local and organic foods are provided in the dining hall.

Environmental Learning Center, Diablo Lake
http://ncascades.org
Phone: (206) 526-2599
Main office in Sedro Wooley (360) 854-2599

Option #3

Diablo Lake Boat Tours

Seattle City Light has been offering Diablo Lake Boat Tours for more than 80 years. After parking at Diablo Lake, a guide will lead you on a short guided walk to the boat dock and talk about some of the area's natural history, biodiversity, and geology. You will learn about the unique relationship between the environment and the three hydroelectric dams, which provide power to the citizens of Seattle.

Diablo Ferry Dock, North End of the Lake

You will board the Cascadian and embark on a cruise of glacier-fed Diablo Lake, to enjoy historic stories about the early explorers and settlers in the area and the formation of the Skagit River Hydroelectric Project. A snack will be provided on board the boat as you learn about the wildlife habitat that surrounds the deep-blue waters of Diablo Lake while enjoying views of glacier-clad peaks, islands, and waterfalls. Tours end with an organic and locally sourced lunch at the North Cascades Environmental Learning Center on the shores of Diablo Lake.

- Tours are offered once a day
- Boat capacity: 40 people
- Check-in begins at 10:45 at North Cascades Environmental Learning Center
- Tours last from 11 a.m. to 2:30 p.m.
- Not wheelchair accessible
- July 2 - Sept. 14 Thurs. - Mon.
- Adults: $40
- Seniors (60 years): $38
- Youth (12 years): $20
- Children (3 years): Free
- **Reservations required**
- Email:skagittours@seattle.gov
- Phone: (360) 854-2589

Along the East Bank Trail
(photo courtesy of National Park Service)

Option #4

East Bank trail (a 16-mile hike from Highway 20 to Lightning Camp)

To access this trail from the south, travel 65 miles along Highway 20 from Burlington past Diablo Lake to milepost 138. From the East Bank Trailhead, it is a short descent to a bridge over Ruby Creek, the scene of a gold rush in the 1880s, with every foot taken up in placer claims. Just across the bridge is a junction with the Canyon Creek Trail; bear left to stay on the East Bank Trail.

At 2.8 miles (4.5 km) there is a trail junction. A short spur trail to Ross Lake and designated campsites goes west, and the steep Little Jack Mountain Trail heads northeast. The main trail goes north, climbing gradually through the forested notch of Hidden Hand Pass. According to miners' stories, Jack Rowley was guided by a pointing hand through this route in 1879 to find gold on Ruby Creek. Jack Mountain is named for Rowley.

Descending through forests for several miles from Hidden Hand Pass, the trail reaches Ross Lake and continues north with fine lake views and opportunities for swimming, camping and fishing along the way. A favourite place to enjoy this lake setting is from the high bridge across the mouth of Devil's Creek Canyon. Lightning Creek camp is reached at 16 miles (26 km) from State Route 20. From here a side trail heads east and steeply upwards toward Desolation Peak. There 5 tent sites at Lightning Creek.

Accommodations

Ross Lake Lodge

Reservations are taken up to a year in advance at 206.386.4437.

Ross Lake Lodge is a rustic floating 12-cabin resort located right on the lake near the Ross Lake dam. The lodge is open from mid-June to October 31. Fishing is open on Ross Lake July 1- October 31. All cabins are equipped for cooking and sleeping. There is no restaurant. The lodge is accessible by the lodge water taxi from the dam. You can rent boats from the lodge or other watercraft.

The fee to take trekkers from the dam up to Lightning Camp is $120, maximum 6 people ($20 per person).

- 14' aluminum or wood boat with a 9.9 horsepower outboard motor. Maximum capacity is five people, less if the boat is loaded with camping equipment. Daily rate is $115.00 + tax
- Discovery Old Towne Canoes - 17 feet, durable plastic with two seats and paddles. Daily rate is $38.00 + tax.
- Eddyline Nighthawk Single Kayak - 16 feet, no dry sacks provided, high stability, light weight plastic. Paddle, spray skirt, and bilge pump included. Daily rate is $50.00 + tax
- Eddyline Whisper Double Kayak - 18 feet, no dry sacks provided, high stability, light weight plastic. Paddles, spray skirt, and bilge pump included. Daily rate is $68.00 + tax

Water taxi rates (**one way**) from the dam to campgrounds on Ross Lake.

Green Point: $25.00

Hidden Hand/Cougar Island: $40.00

Big Beaver: $60.00

Devils Junction: $95.00

Lightning Creek: $115.00

Desolation: $120.00

Little Beaver: $135.00

Silver Creek/Hozomeen: $175.00

Highway 20 Road conditions - http://www.wsdot.wa.gov/traffic/passes/northcascades/
North Cascades Highway (Hwy 20) Hotline 1-360-707-5055
Permits: National Park Service, Marblemount
7280 Ranger Station Rd., Marblemount
http://www.nps.gov/noca/planyourvisit/visitorcenters.htm

Drive Hwy 20 toward Marblemount and turn onto Ranger Station Road, which leaves Hwy 20 at milepost 105.3, just west of Marblemount, and drive 0.7 miles to the end of the road and the ranger station. The station has exhibits about wilderness and backcountry travel. There's a great relief map. You can make sales of books, maps, and other items related to wilderness, hiking, and climbing.

This centre is the main backcountry permit office for North Cascades National Park and the adjacent Ross Lake and Lake Chelan National Recreation Areas. Ask for help at the information desk. Backcountry permits are required year-round and are available at an outdoor self-issue station when the station is closed.

THE AUTHOR, MICHAEL MCCARTHY

I blame everything on Jack. I was a teenager in Montreal when I came across a copy of On the Road. I think it was compulsory to read it in our English Literature class. Like many other people ranging from Bob Dylan to Jim Morrison have also claimed, *On the Road* changed my life.

I don't know what it is about Kerouac's writing that affected so many people. Sure it was the rebellion against normalcy, a rejection of conformity, a burning desire to live life the way you wanted to and not the way you were told. Maybe it was Kerouac's embracement of black culture, like jazz. Or his affection for the downtrodden, the working man, the ordinary guy. Or maybe it was just the urge to move, to wander, to explore. As Robert Louis Stevenson wrote, the essence of travel is simply to be on the move. Or, as the old cliché has it, it's the journey and not the destination that truly matters.

I lived in a suburb that didn't have bus access across the Victoria Bridge to downtown Montreal. By the time I was 14 I was old enough to take the bus on my own, but there was no bus. So, after reading *On the Road*, I started to stick out my thumb. The highway was only a block away from my house. In those days, there were no worries about murderers and sex predators and psychotics driving cars. You stuck out your thumb and within a few minutes some kindly soul would stop and away you went.

After a few years of hitching into Montreal, I started to expand my territory, hitching further afield within the province of Quebec. By my late teens I was hitching across Canada, from Montreal several thousand kilometres to Vancouver. I forgot how many times I did that epic trek, both directions. On one journey, heading west from Montreal, there seemed to be no other hitchhikers on the road. I quickly travelled through Ontario until I got to Brandon, Manitoba, where I discovered where all my competition had gone. Some doofus driving a school bus had picked up every hitchhiker he saw, over 50 of them, and dumped them all when he finished his trip in Brandon.

With 50 people hitching on the side of the road, soon there was a huge backlog, and the police were called in, and a temporary hostel set up in the form of a tent, and only 6 people were allowed to hitch at one time. So it was a week's wait just to be allowed to stick out your thumb. A couple of us hippies decided it was time to start hopping freights. We crept down to the freight yard, bided our time, watched for the "bulls" who guarded the tracks, and jumped aboard.

Hopping freights proved to be a dangerous exercise, and whenever I had the money I would "ride the hound" instead, buying cheap tickets on Greyhound buses. I took the passenger train 3 times across the whole country. Eventually I left Canada entirely, riding the hound all across the U.S. starting in New York and stopping in Washington, Baltimore, St. Louis, Oklahoma City, Albuquerque and Los Angeles. In Oklahoma City, I finally ran out of money and food. I went to the police station to see if I could be arrested for vagrancy and thereby secure a hot meal. The police just laughed and drove me to the Sally Ann, where I had the privilege of singing Rock of Ages for my dinner, a boiled egg and a piece of stale white toast.

Over a course of several years I slept in fields, the bottom of telephone booths, back alleys, church pews, and wherever I could find a bed. Eventually I ended up sleeping on a couch in a hippie commune in Vancouver, where I earned my keep washing dishes and cleaning up. After several months I worked my way onto welfare and a bed on the floor. In the basement the local anarchists ran a printing press where they pumped out subversive literature and underground poetry. Kerouac would have loved it.

As I write this, it has been exactly 50 years since I first hit the road and I've been on the road ever since. I've travelled to 25 countries and enjoyed several hundred adventures ranging from swimming with great white sharks to socializing with the wildlife in the Galapagos. I've trekked across the Himalayas and been captured by Maoist guerrillas. My damned ferryboat almost sank in a giant lake full of crocodiles in Cambodia. I've snuck into several prisons without permission, and slept in more fleabags than I care to remember.

I blame it all on Jack. My wanderlust is directly a consequence of his carrying that silly roll of teletype paper containing his manuscript – his masterpiece – for so many years until he found a publisher crazy enough to publish it. There's certainly something to be said for perseverance. If you happen to have that particular quality, take a hike up Desolation Peak in the North Cascades Wilderness and pay your respects to a crazy guy who helped change the world. If you find the 12,000-foot ascent and descent to be a tad difficult, blame Jack. I don't think he would give a damn.

Michael McCarthy
Vancouver, Canada
2015

CPSIA information can be obtained at www.ICGtesting.com
Printed in the USA
LVIW01n1204260818
588184LV00016B/1099